you have sweet dreams.
— Bobbi McPeak-Bailey

Sweet Dreams

a Garden Lullaby

Story by Bobbi McPeak-Bailey   Illustrated by Deborah DeFazio

WEE PRESS

THE WEE PRESS • Terre Haute, Indiana • Zionsville, Indiana

Published by The Wee Press
P.O. Box 367: Zionsville, Indiana 46077
or
P.O. Box 3221: Terre Haute, Indiana 47803

Most men, on the other hand, act on a week-to-week, month-to-month basis as if deeply knowing and being known is something to be avoided at all costs. I am frankly not sure where this fear comes from. I do know that deep down most men find knowing and being known just as pleasurable as women. When something calamitous happens and the man is forced into sharing himself and taking in his woman, he experiences a deep pleasure and asks himself why he waited so long. But the same man often goes right back to avoiding this kind of intimate contact on a day-to-day basis like the plague. Many women grow tired of this imbalance and give up.

My advice is not revolutionary. Patience. A willingness to wait for opportunities. Talking about the pleasure of real contact when it occurs so learning seeps in.

Good luck and here is an excerpt from a poem I like, that relates to this, by *William Stafford*:

"If you don't know the kind of person I am and I don't know the kind of person you are a pattern that others made may prevail in the world and following the wrong god home we miss our star. For there is many a small betrayal in the mind, a shrug that lets the fragile sequence break sending with shouts the horrible errors of childhood storming out to play through the broken dike."

Contributing Writer

Robert Swain

I am not a frog! Let's make this clear from the beginning. Though I must confess that at times in my life I may have croaked and ate flies and even hopped around a little, I am not a frog.

Strong willed, driven and destined for glory, you have not only grown into the roles of leadership and power but also made homes for our children. I salute you. Without your efforts over the last few centuries the Black population of the country would be nothing. As your standards raise, individually and as a group, you look for a mate that will at least be your equal. This can be no easy task considering the challenges facing black men in America today.

Many of you end up having to settle for a brother that you hope has the capabilities to live up to the "potential" that you see in him. This is your frog. Not really the man, but your idea of what he could be. You say, "All I have to do is kiss him." Yeah, that may work for a moment but he still is who he is. You then find out that you have to keep kissing and kissing and kissing him, trying to keep your dreams and his "potential" from fading into reality. It is not hard to see how tired and frustrated you both can become. Eventually you find a new frog to kiss. It is a never-ending story.

How do we (and I say "we" because we Princes are waiting for you) solve this problem? I believe there are three basic things that have to be done:

• First and foremost we have to become "fully" spiritually aware. Fully means we have to learn to live the ways of our maker. It means to be at peace with ourselves, learning how to love and be loved. Too often we look at the worldly aspects (sex, money, material things.) of a relationship as the basis for its growth. Although these are important, they are not the foundation on which

Thanks Sue Ann

and

For children and parents everywhere
who love to read together anywhere - B.M.B.

For my Lord, family and friends - D.D.

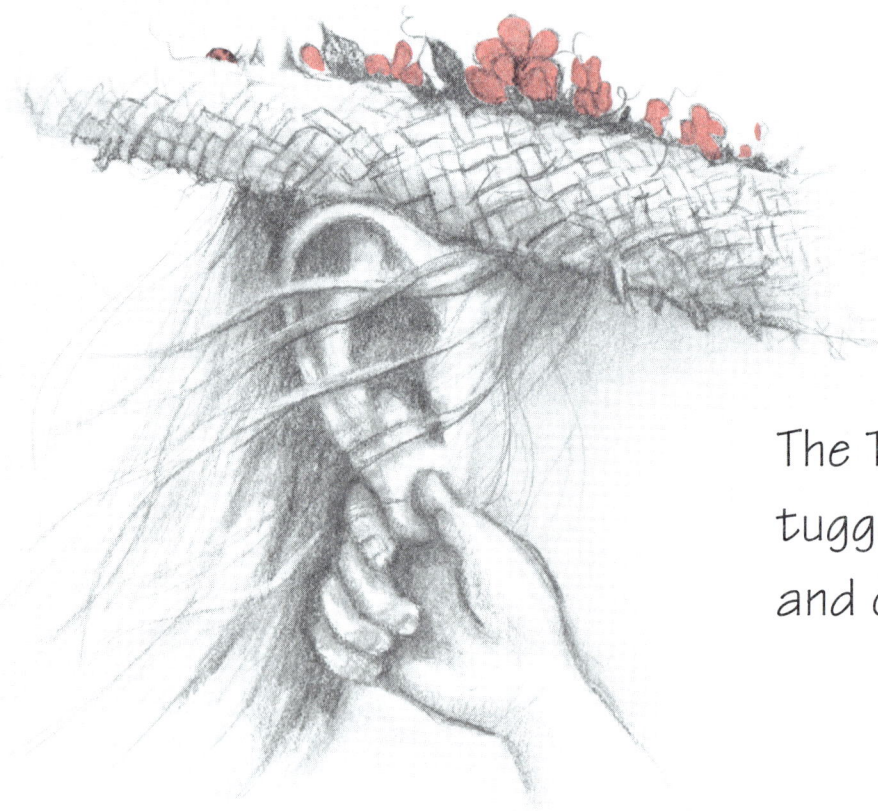

The Tired Little One
tugged mama's ear lobe
and chanted ever so sleepily,

"Read just one more book....just one more book..."

"That is what you said after
the last book!" reminded mama,
gently rocking the worn
wicker porch swing

back and forth,
back and forth.

"P-l-e-a-s-e!...

If you don't

read me another book,"

teased the Tired One...

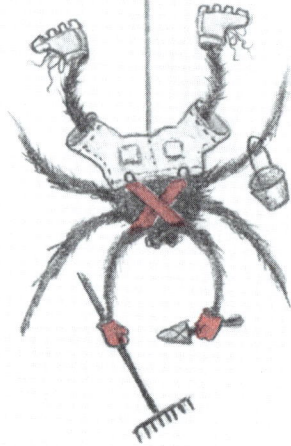

"I'm going
to be a big
brown spider
like the one
I saw in your
garden
and crawl
up your arm!"

"What!"
exclaimed mama.
"You are too beautiful to be a spindly spider.

Tomorrow why don't you be a ballerina and dance with my dahlias?"

"No! I'd
rather be
a strong
wind and...

...knock down
your daisies!"

"You're too gentle for that," said mama.

"Why not skip with the sun and the wind, scattering wildflower seeds?"

"Not me!
I'll be a bumble bee
and buzz around your ears!"

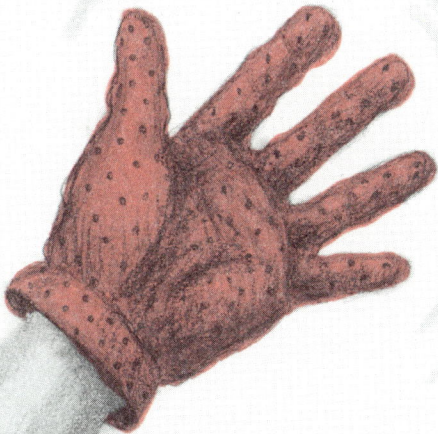

"You are much too polite
to be a pesky bumble bee
buzzing about my head....

Why don't you be a little
ladybug and bask in the
early morning sunlight?"
said mama.

"I don't want to do that," said the Tired One.

"I want to be a storm and rain until your flowers are all wet and tangled."

"Be a soft little summer shower and go pity-pat on my garden.

My seedlings will grow straight and tall," said mama.

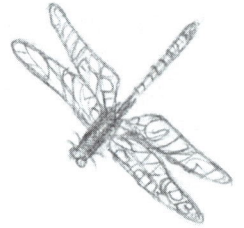

"Nope," declared the Tired One.

"I'm going to be a caterpillar and eat up your green garden!"

"Please don't be
a caterpillar
and eat my
green garden,"
said mama.

"Tomorrow be a bright butterfly and gather sweet nectar from my rainbow of flowers!"

"W-e-l-l maybe I'll j-just

p-pick your f-flowers..."

said the Sleepy One.

"Why?" asked mama.
"So I can give them to y-you,"
said the Almost Sleeping One.

Up from the porch swing mama lifted her
and into the house they went.

"Good night little ray
of dancing sunshine,"
whispered mama as she
tucked the Sleeping One
in her warm bed.

"Sleep tight my gentle rain,"
added mama as she kissed
the Sleeping One's forehead.

"Sweet dreams beautiful seedling,"

said mama just so softly as she
tip-toed to the door.

Cabbage

Sweet Dreams

SLEEP
TIGHT

SWEET
POTATO

Turnips

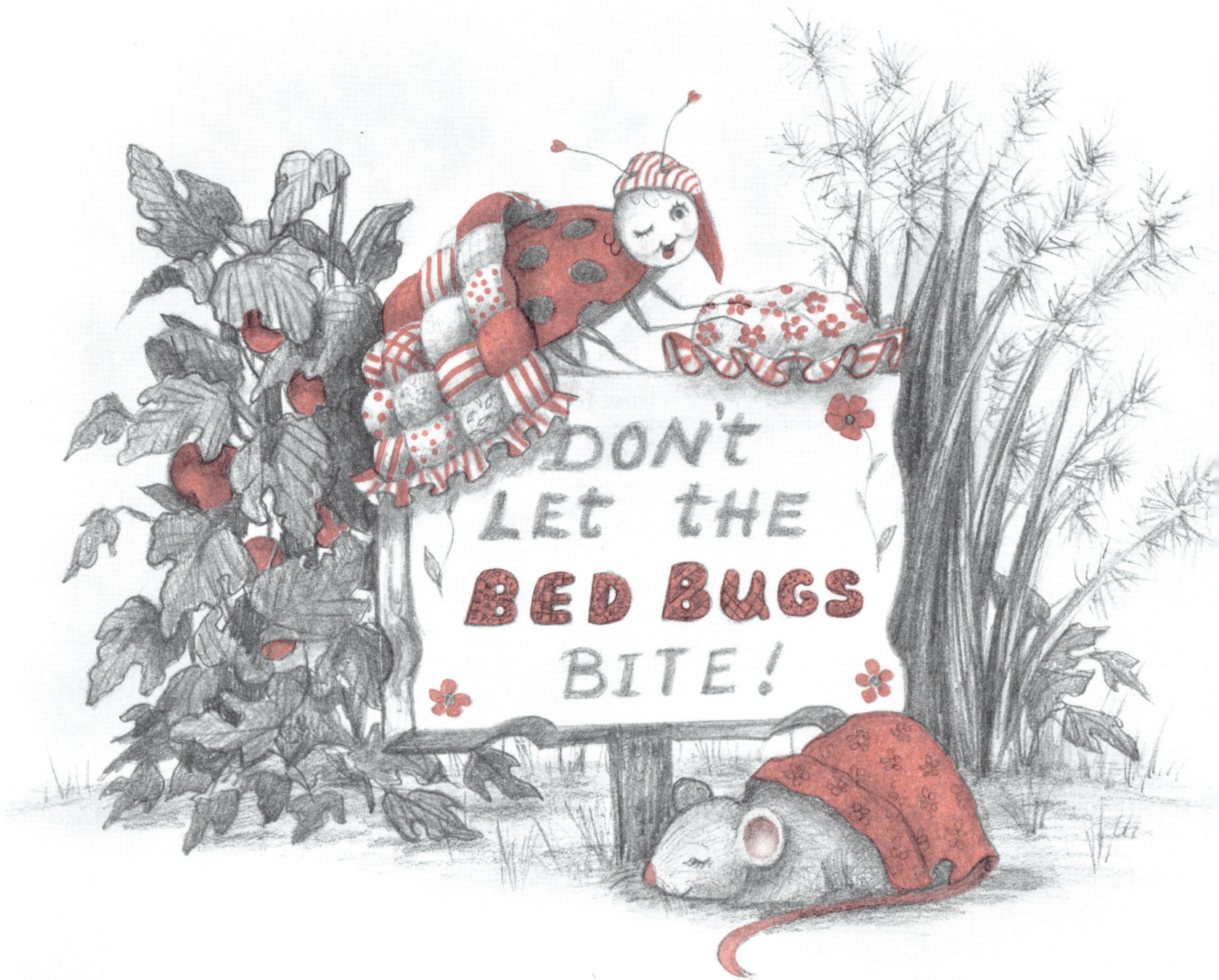

DON'T LET THE BED BUGS BITE!